Monographic Journals of the Near East   *Afroasiatic Linguistics* 3/4 (September 1976)

SCHWA INSERTION IN BERBER: [1] *UN PROBLEME DE CHOIX*

by

Jilali Saib

Department of Linguistics
University of California, Los Angeles

The question of whether schwas are inserted or present in underlying representations of C_1C_2 and $C_1C_2C_3$ verb stems in Berber is examined here in detail. This examination consists of proposing, motivating, and evaluating a number of analyses possible within the generative framework. It also considers recent proposals concerning "abstractness" and "concreteness" of underlying representations, and alternative orderings of phonological rules. It is concluded that a "totally concrete" analysis — i.e. with underlying schwas — is superior to other less concrete ones, chief among them the "totally abstract analysis" — with consonants only. The implications of this conclusion are discussed and suggestions for further research are made.

TABLE OF CONTENTS

		page
	TABLE OF CONTENTS	1
1.	INTRODUCTION: THE PROBLEM	2
2.	THE ANALYSES	3
	2.1. The totally abstract analysis	3
	2.2. The Randomly Ordered Rules Abstract Analysis	7
	2.3. The totally concrete analysis	8
	2.4. The intermediate analyses	11
3.	CONCLUSION	12
	BIBLIOGRAPHY	12

[1] This paper grew out of research begun in the Fall of 1972. In preparing it I have benefited from insightful discussions with Professors Victoria Fromkin and Larry Hyman; I am grateful for their help and their encouragements. I would also like to thank Professors Bedell, Givon, Penchoen, Johnson, and Mickey Noonan for their comments on an earlier draft of this paper. Any errors or omissions are my sole responsibility, however. An abridged version of this paper was presented at the 5th Annual Conference on African Linguistics, Stanford University (March 1974).

1. INTRODUCTION: THE PROBLEM

One of the most intriguing problems in Berber phonology concerns the status and behavior of schwa. As seen in (1),

(1) *i* *u*

a

most Berber languages, spoken throughout North Africa, have a simple underlying vowel system. However, on the surface, a fourth vowel,[2] schwa, occurs with great frequency. In fact, certain verbs, which are given in their citation form[3] in (2) have only schwa:

(2) [əxðəm] 'to work' [əns] 'to wear'
[əzðəɣ] 'to dwell' [ḍər] 'to go down'

This fourth vowel differs from the three vowels in (1) in that its occurrence is restricted. As exemplified in (3), the other vowels occur in both closed and open syllables, while schwa occurs only in closed syllables:[4]

(3)	closed syllable		open syllable	
	[aš]	'to you'	[ša]	'something'
	[əš]	'to give'	*[šə]	

Moreover, the exact position of schwas is totally predictable. Returning, for example, to the phonetic verb forms in (2), we note, as indicated in (4), that schwa occurs either before a word-final consonant or before two consonants (or a geminate):[5]

---

[2] The question of whether this schwa arises historically through vowel reduction as is the case in a great many languages (e.g. classical Arabic *kataba*, Moroccan Arabic [əktəb] 'he wrote'), or is an underlying vowel in its own right is a very interesting question but one which I will not take up here. The problem of schwa and all the questions related to it will be taken up in detail in my forthcoming Doctoral Dissertation.

[3] In Berber the Citation Form which happens to be the Imperative Singular, is the least morphologically marked form. The data presented here are given in broad phonetic transcription. A dot under a consonant indicates that that consonant is pharyngealized.

[4] The data presented in this paper from Tamaziɣt (Ait Ndhir). One Berber language to which this statement will not apply is Twareg, which according to De Foucauld [1920] later confirmed by Prasse [1960:58-60], does exhibit instances of CəCV (e.g. *tenəɣe* 'act of killing', cf. Tamaziɣt *θinɣi*), and of CəCə (e.g. *ekəbər* 'hill'). The only instances of CəCV in other Berber languages (e.g. Tamaziɣt *xəmməm+ən* → [xəmməmən] 'they reflected on'), are actually not counter-examples. I have a principled explanation for them: the second ə of the stem, which should have been deleted, is maintained to keep the *m*'s apart. In my dialect, deletion takes place in fast speech and the result is the absorption of the third *m* by the geminate, yielding [xəmmən] with a strong geminate *m*.

[5] This is in accordance with my paper on geminates (Saib [1973]) where it is argued that, at least in Berber, geminates are to be treated as a sequence of two identical segments. A convention whereby they will be redundantly specified as [+tense] is also proposed.

(4) /___C#

/___CC

Since the occurrence and exact position of schwa can be predicted, it is possible to maintain that there are no schwas in underlying representations for the surface verb forms in (2). Instead, they would consist simply of three and two consonants, as in (5):

(5) /xðm/ 'to work' /ns/ 'to wear'

/zðγ/ 'to dwell' /ḍr/ 'to go down'

It is to be noted that the underlying forms in (5) are similar to those posited for verb stems in Semitic languages (cf. the treatment of Arabic and Hebrew verbs, for example.) In dealing with stems like those in (5), generations of Berberists (Laoust [1918], Basset [1929] and [1952], Abdel Massih [1968], and Penchoen [1973] simply adopted the Semitists' approach and regarded the consonants to be the "truss" of the stems. As Basset [1952:11] put it: "Un groupement exclusif de consonnes constitue le radical et, partant, l'armature sémantique du mot."

As for the schwas, they are said to be inserted according to consonant clustering, which is in turn based on the nature of the consonants. Thus, in /C_1C_2/ stems, for instance, the following clusterings are observed (cf. Laoust [1918]): if C_1 is [sonorant], and C_2 is [+sonorant], clustering is prohibited, and a [ə] is inserted between C_1 and C_2 (e.g. /ḍr/ 'to go down' is realized as [ḍər] not *[əḍr]: and /gn/ 'to sleep' as [gən] not *[əgn]. If on the other hand C_1 is [+son] and C_2 is not, clustering is allowed (e.g. /ls/ 'to wear' is pronounced [als] not *[ləs]; and /nz/ 'to be sold' [ənz], not *[nəz].

To discuss the inadequacies of this approach would take us too far afield. Suffice it to say that: (i) consonant clustering varies from one Berber language to another, from one speaker to another, and even within the speech of one speaker; (ii) if followed strictly, this approach will force one to end up, as did Abdel Massih [1968:25-26], with incorrect or, at best, very questionable forms like these: *[nəs] 'to spend the night', *[hədəm] 'to demolish', *[fərəḥ] 'to be happy'.

Returning now to the main discussion, we find that, in addition to positing underlying forms like those in (5), there would have to be a rule (or rules) of schwa insertion operating in the environments given earlier in (4). In the remainder of this paper I shall first explore the theoretical implications of the analysis just outlined, which I will call the "totally abstract" analysis. After pointing out certain objections one might raise against this approach, I shall then present a second analysis which avoids the shortcomings of the first. But before continuing, a word on what is meant by "abstract" and "concrete" is in order. These terms are used in this paper to indicate the distance from / / to [ ]. Since the underlying forms in (5) are far removed from their surface realizations, an analysis which posits them would be "totally abstract." In contrast, an analysis which posits, as underlying forms, forms like those in (2) would be a "totally concrete" one, since they are exactly identical to their phonetic shape or representation.

2. THE ANALYSES

2.1. The Totally Abstract Analysis

In the "totally abstract" analysis a rule like the one in (6) is needed to take us from abstract underlying forms like those in (5) to the surface forms given in (2):[6]

[6]Rule (6) is written in this way so as to account for all the so-called vowel-less verb stems, be they /C/ (cf. [əš] in (3)), /$C_1C_2C_3$/, or /C_1C_2/ (cf. (5) above), though an extra

(6) $\phi \rightarrow ə / \{\#, C\}$ ------- $C \begin{Bmatrix} \# \\ C \end{Bmatrix}$ (i) (ii)

(Condition: Directionality[7] of application: right-to-left, counting segments).

Notice two things. First, the subparts of the rule must be extrinsically ordered, and the directionality of their application must be right-to-left, counting segments. A sample derivation is given in (7):

(7) /#xð m#/ 'to work'

xðəm (by 6i)

əxðəm (by 6ii)

[əxðəm]

As seen in (8a-b), failure to observe the two conditions just mentioned leads to incorrect surface forms:

(8) a. Wrong ordering, correct directionality:

/#x ð m#/

x əð m (by 6ii)

xəðəm (by 6i)

*[xəðəm]

b. Right ordering, wrong directionality:

/# x ð m#]

əx ð m (by 6ii, 6i inapplicable)

əx əð m (by 6ii)

əxəðəm (by 6i)

*[əxəðəm]

In (8a) an incorrect output is obtained because the subparts of the rule are applied in the wrong order but with the correct directionality. In (8b) the subparts of the rules are applied in the right order but with the wrong directionality. Again the output is incorrect.

The second fact about this analysis is that it requires that we distinguish between two different word-internal grammatical boundaries (+ and #) for the suffixes. As seen in (9), the + boundary has no effect on the application of rule (6):[8]

---

rule of SCHWA MOVEMENT (or SCHWA HOPPING) is needed in order to obtain the correct phonetic output of certain /C_1C_2/ stems especially those containing sonorants. That this is so, one might note, should not be too alarming, as these stems have been observed to behave strangely in other languages with respect to epenthesis. Mickey Noonan, now at San Jose State University, informs me (personal communication) that this was the case in Pre-Indo-European, as reconstructed by Lehmann [1952:112-113] (i.e. with Obstruents, Resonants, Laryngeals and a "non-segmental" phone /ʌ/, syllabicity). Nevertheless, certain /C_1C_2/ stems remain a distinct problem for a "totally abstract" analysis.

[7] For a detailed discussion of Directionality and the "Directional theory," see Johnson [1970] and Howard [1973] and the references cited there.

[8] The complete list of the personal subject affixes is the following: (to be compared to those in (19))

(9) /#x ð m+ x#/   'I worked'

x ð m ə x   (by 6i)

xəðm ə x   (by 6ii)

[xəðm ə x]

While the correct form for the first person singular is obtained in (9), an incorrect output is observed in most dialects for the second person singular, as seen in (10):

(10) /#θ+x ð m+ ð#/   'you (sing.) worked'   (wrong boundary)

θ x ð m əð

θ xəðm əð

əθ xəðm əð

*[əθ xəðm əð]

In order to obtain the correct output, a stronger boundary is required before the suffix /ð/ and an even stronger boundary, ##, after it.

(11) /#θ+ x ð m#ð##/   'you (sing.) worked'   (correct boundaries)

θ+ xðəm#ð##   (by 6i)

θ xðəm#ð##   (by 6ii)

[θ əxðəmð]

Other suffixes which, likewise, require an internal word boundary and the stronger boundary ## are the second and third person feminine plural given in (12) and (13):

(12) /# θ+x ðm+ m#θ##/[9]   'you (fem. plur.) worked'

θ+x ðm+əm#θ##

θ+xəðm ə #θ##

θ+xəðm ə #θ##

[əθ xəðm ə m θ]

1.	______x	1.	*n*______
2.	θ______	2m.	θ______*m*
3m.	*i*______	2f.	θ______*m*θ
3f.	θ______	3m.	______*n*
		3f.	______*n*θ

They are listed here without boundaries so as not to prejudice the issues. It should be noted however, that the /θ/ in the plural suffixes is the feminine marker (cf. also the feminine noun formation: e.g. masc. *amaziγ* 'Berber man'; fem. θ-*amaziγ*-θ 'Berber woman.')

[9]The strong boundary ## in (11) - (13) is needed to insure that rule (6) will not insert a ə before the simple suffix /ð/ and the /θ/ of the complex suffixes /-mθ/ and /-nθ/ which will result in incorrect surface forms. While some dialects allow the insertion of ə before /ð/, no dialect allows such an insertion before the /θ/ of the complex suffixes.

(13) /# x ð m+ n#θ##/ 'They (fem.) worked'
x ð m+ən#θ## (by 6i)
xəðm ən#θ## (by 6ii)
[xə ðmə n θ]

Again, if a + boundary is posited instead of an internal word boundary, the wrong output is obtained as seen in (14) and (15):

(14) /#θ +x ð m+m+ θ#/ 'you (fem. plur.) worked'
θ +x ð m+m+əθ (by 6i)
θ +xðəm+m+əθ (by 6ii)
θə+xðəm+m+əθ (by 6ii)
*[θə xðə mmə θ]

(15) /# x ð m+ n+ θ#/ 'They (fem.) worked'
x ð m+ n ə θ (by 6i)
xðəm+ n ə θ (by 6ii)
ə+xðəm+ n ə θ (by 6ii)
*[əxðə mnəθ]

Since the problematic suffixes involve [ð] and [θ] (i.e. [+anterior, +coronal, +continuent, -strident] segments), one might argue that one way of solving the problem — and hence salvage the "Totally Abstract Analysis" — would be by stating the environment of rule (6) so as to exclude these segments. It should be noted, however, that this restriction would further complicate the already complicated environment of the rule. Moreover, a further restriction making use of + would be required, viz.,

$$/ \_\_\_ + \underset{[F's]}{C} \left\{ \begin{array}{l} \# \quad \text{(i)} \\ \begin{bmatrix} +C \\ F's \end{bmatrix} \quad \text{(ii)} \end{array} \right\}$$

as Berber has verb stems ending in /ð/ and /θ/ (e.g. [ənɣəð] 'to become finer'; [əwwəθ] 'to hit'.)

But although this abstract analysis can be made to account for the data, it leaves one with a great deal of uneasiness. Indeed, several objections can be raised against it. For one thing, it posits unnatural and unpronounceable underlying forms, like those in (5), for the stems given in (2). One might rightly question the necessity of positing such abstract underlying forms since Berber has other verb stems WITH vowels (e.g. [fafa] 'to wake up', (-trans.); [aðu] 'to fold'). Thus, the underlying forms in (2) seem to break the pattern of Berber morphemes.[10] However, even if one could derive all vowels in all verb stems in the language,

---

[10]It might be argued, of course, that it is these stems which break the pattern. However, the statistics bear my statement out. According to De Foucauld, quoted in Basset's Introduction, [1929], out of a total of 1400 Twareg verbs, 400 stems are of the $/C_1C_2C_3/$ type, while 50 stems are of the $/C_1C_2/$ type. This is including borrowings from Arabic, most of which are of the first type. Moreover, a great many verbs belonging to the basic core vocabulary have plain vowels.

we might still question the motivation for setting up such abstract underlying forms. In addition, the assignment of different boundaries to certain affixes is in itself an inconsistency which makes this analysis look very ad hoc. It is ad hoc, first, because of the arbitrariness of boundary assignment. There is no grammatical basis for assigning a + boundary in the case of certain personal affixes, but internal word boundaries for other personal affixes. In addition, this boundary assignment is circular: there is no other phonological process rule in the language which distinguishes between a + boundary and an internal word boundary #, as would the rule of schwa insertion in this "totally abstract" analysis, nor is there a rule calling for such a liberal use of boundaries.

Moreover, the "totally abstract" analysis, as was pointed out above (cf. fn. 6) does not handle certain /C_1C_2/ stems without difficulty. If the correct phonetic output of verbs like [ǰən] 'to sleep' and [səɣ] 'to buy' can be obtained by the simple application of the first part of rule (6) to underlying /ǰn/ and /sɣ/ it is not so for others; viz. /nz/ 'to be sold' → [ənz], not *[nəz]; /rs/'to settle' → [ərs], not *[rəs]; /ẓð̣/ 'to grind' → [əẓð̣], not *[ẓəð̣]. An extra rule of "schwa movement" or "schwa hopping" — the environment of which is highly restricted — is needed in order to get the correct surface forms for these verbs. Such a MINOR RULE is clearly ad hoc since its SOLE function is to "fix up" incorrect outputs yielded by the application of (6i) to certain /C_1C_2/ stems. Its ad hoc-ness adds to the cost of the "totally abstract" analysis. Alternatives to the addition of an extra rule, for example marking these stems with a [-Rule X] feature (in this case (6i)) in the lexicon, are not satisfactory either, as they are just as ad hoc and just as costly.

Finally, even the extrinsic ordering constraint[11] can be dispensed with, as is discussed below, and can be replaced by a random sequential application of the subparts of rule (6). This is particularly interesting in that it suggests that, at least in some cases, the No-Extrinsic Ordering Hypothesis currently advocated by some phonologists (Vennemann [1972]; Hooper [1973], Koutsoudas et al [1974]), can be a viable alternative.

Thus, there exists an equally abstract alternative to the "totally abstract analysis A," which I will call "The Randomly Ordered Rules Abstract Analysis."

2.2. The Randomly Ordered Rules Abstract Analysis

In this analysis the subparts of the rule of schwa insertion given in (6) can apply randomly (i.e. unordered) provided there is, in addition, a "corrective" rule of schwa deletion as stated in (16):

(16) ə → ∅ / ____ CV

As seen in (17), the same underlying form uniquely yields the correct output by application of rules (6) and (16) in any order and in any direction:

(17) a.	/#θ+xðm+ m#θ##/	'You (fem. plur.) worked'
	θ+xðm+əm#θ##	(by 6i)
	əθ+xðm+əm#θ##	(by 6ii)
	əθ+xəðm+əm#θ##	(by 6ii)
	[əθxəðməmθ]	

[11]Talmy Givon (personal communication) suggested to me that another possible formal way of achieving this would be by giving the # in the right hand side of the environment the value of a consonant. What would follow from this suggestion is that the closed syllable would be ___CC or ___C#. I have not had the time to evaluate this suggestion but will investigate its consequences in my dissertation.

(In (17a.) the rules are applied first to the suffix, then to the prefix, then to the stem.)

(17) b. /#θ +x ð m+ m#θ##

θ +xðəm+ m#θ## (by 6ii)

θə+xðəm+ m#θ## (by 6ii)

θə+xðəm+əm#θ## (by 6i)

θə+x ð m+əm#θ## (by 16)

θə+xəðm+əm#θ## (by 6ii)

θ +xəðm+əm#θ## (by 16)

əθ +xəðm+əm#θ## (by 6ii)

[əθ xəð mə m θ]

(In (17b.) the rules are applied to the stem, then to the prefix, then to the suffix.)

It should be pointed out that the rule stated in (16), though it was referred to as a "corrective rule," is actually not an ad-hoc one. It simply takes advantage of the general constraint on the restricted occurrence of schwas exemplified in (3). It guarantees that no schwas will occur in an open syllable.

But this alternative analysis, though it does not require extrinsic rule ordering, still suffers from the other pitfalls of the "totally abstract" analysis, namely the ABSTRACTNESS of the underlying forms and the AD HOC USE of boundaries. This brings us to another alternative analysis, this time a "totally concrete" one.

2.3. The Totally Concrete Analysis

The "abstract" analyses A and B just presented can be said to be motivated by a principle which plays an important role in the S.P.E. type of phonology (Chomsky and Halle [1968]): the principle of eliminating, as much as is feasible, redundancy from the lexicon. That is, things which can be predictable by rule should not be included in the underlying forms. However, we have just seen certain difficulties which can result from the strict application of this principle to the Berber schwa situation.

Now what about the "totally concrete analysis"? This analysis is, likewise, motivated by general principles. First, the phonetic shape of the least morphologically marked form tends to be chosen as the underlying form (cf. Greenberg [1966]; Vennemann [1972]). Second, the principle of minimization of the difference between underlying representation and phonetic representation (i.e. redundancy does not matter) (cf. Hale [1971], as reported in Kiparsky [1971]; Vennemann [1972] and [1973]; Hooper [1973]). Third, the principle of No-Extrinsic Rule Ordering (cf. Koutsoudas et al [1971]; Vennemann [1972]; Hooper [1973]). Thus, according to this concrete approach, forms like the ones given in (2) will appear as given in (18):

(18)	/əxðəm/	'to work'	[xðəm]
	/əzðəɣ/	'to dwell'	[əzðəɣ]
	/əns/	'to wear'	[əns]
	/ḍər/	'to go down'	[ḍər]

(i.e. identical to their phonetic shape).

As seen in (19), affixes will appear with vocalic support. (As for the reason why /-ð/ does not appear with a ə, cf. fn. 9).

(19) PERSONAL SUBJECT AFFIXES

	SINGULAR			PLURAL	
1.	________	+əx	1.	nə+________	
2.	θə+________	+ð	2m.	θə+________	+əm
3m.	*i* +________		2f.	θə+________	+əm+θ
3f.	θə+________		3m.	________	+ən
			3f.	________	+ən+θ

(Where *m* = masculine; and *f* = feminine.)

It should be pointed out that by positing the forms in (19), I am not replacing boundaries with schwas so as to avoid problems. The positing of affixes with schwas is in accordance with the second general principle motivating the "totally concrete" analysis. Moreover, a look at the Berber data presented here as well as other data will indicate that, at the surface level, affixes — with the exception of /-ð/ (cf. fn. 9 however) — appear with vocalic support.

For the sake of reference, the full preterit conjugation of the verb 'to work' is given in (20):

(20)

		UNDERLYING		PHONETIC
		/əxðəm/		[əxðəm]
sg.	1.	əxðəm+əx	1.	[xəðməx]
	2.	θə+əxðəm+ð	2.	[θəxðəmð]
	3m.	*i*+əxðəm	3m.	[ixðəm]
	3f.	θə+əxðəm	3f.	[θəxðəm]
pl.	1.	nə+əxðəm	1.	[nəxðəm]
	2m.	θə+əxðəm+əm	2m.	[əθxəðməm]
	2f.	θə+əxðəm+əm+θ	2f.	[əθxəðməmθ]
	3m.	əxðəm+ən	3m.	[xəðmən]
	3f.	əxðəm+ən+θ	3f.	[xəðmənθ]

In (20), we see that most forms require no more than the addition of the affixes and the low level phonetic rule of vowel deletion (or absorption) given in (21):[12]

(21) ə → ∅ / V

Only a few forms require the application of the major rules given in (22) and (23):

(22) ə → ∅ / --- C V

---

[12]It should be pointed out that rule (12) is by no means an ad-hoc rule as it is found to be operative in other languages. It is similar, for instance, to the elision of a schwa in front of another vowel in French (e.g. /lə # aRbR/ → [laRbR] 'the tree'.)

(23) ∅ → ə / --- C C V[13]

(Again, geminates = C_XC_X, i.e. a sequence).

Given the underlying forms in (18) and rules (21), (22) and (23), the derivation of the phonetic forms for the first person singular and the second person feminine plural would be that given in (24):

(24)a.	1ST PERSON SINGULAR		(24)b.	2ND PERSON FEM. PLURAL	
	/#əxðəm+əx#/			/#θə+əxðəm+ m+θ#/	
	əx ð m ə x	(by 22)		θə+əx ð m ə m θ	(by 22)
	əxə ðm ə x	(by 23)		θ əx ð m ə m θ	(by 21)
	xə ðm ə x	(by 22)		θ əxə ðm ə m θ	(by 23)
	[xə ðm ə x]			θ xə ðm ə m θ	(by 22)
				əθ xə ðm ə m θ	(by 23)
				[əθ xə ð mə m θ]	

It should be noted that: first, unlike analyses A and B, the "totally concrete" analysis does not require the use of morpheme boundaries for only certain affixes, a practice which we have indicated to be very questionable. Second, unlike analysis A, it does not require extrinsic rule ordering. Third, the rules it requires are both natural and needed in the grammar anyway (especially (23)). And fourth, unlike the other analyses, it does not run into any difficulty with respect to the /C_1C_2/ stems (cf. fn. 6 and the discussion on p. 7): they are simply listed in the lexicon with their vowel in its appropriate place (cf. (2) and (18)).

Two consequences follow from the "totally concrete" analysis. First, it requires redundant information in the lexical representation of formatives, since it has been shown that one can predict the phonetic occurrences of schwas. If this is the correct solution, it implies that speakers, in learning the grammar of their language, do not make all the possible generalizations which the data would permit. That is, it implies that rather than constructing very complex rules the speaker will store formatives with underlying segments which could be predicted. It may also imply that, instead of storing complicated rules, native speakers learn patterns; which is what traditional grammarians have said all along.[14] We do not at present have any ways of testing this hypothesis; nor does the proposed evaluation metric permit us to fully compare complexity of rules in relation to complexity in the lexicon.

Second, this analysis shows that given less abstract representation extrinsic ordering is not necessary. The current debate regarding the No-Extrinsic Rule Ordering Hypothesis is far from settled (cf. Campbell [1973]). It is still not clear how one is to evaluate the consequences of constraining the ordering of rules in a grammar. It is clear, however, that where extrinsic ordering is disallowed, certain generalizations concerning predictable surface forms are lost, at least in this Berber case.

The theoretical implications of the analyses of schwa in Berber are summarized in the chart given in (25):

---

[13]Notice that since the environment is not stated as in (6) no directionality is needed.

[14]An attempt to test whether Berber speakers store formatives like those in (2) as given in (5) or as given in (18), or whether they learn patterns, is envisaged for my forthcoming Doctoral Dissertation.

(25)

	Analysis A	Analysis B	Analysis C
Lexical Redundancy	NO	NO	YES
Rule Redundancy	NO	YES	YES
Rule Ordering	Extrinsic	Intrinsic*	Intrinsic
Directionality	R to L**	NO	NO

(Where: * Intrinsic in analysis B = random sequential ordering
** R to L: right to left (extrinsic))

There are further problems, since, in addition to the "totally abstract" and "totally concrete" analyses there are demonstrably a myriad of "compromise" of "intermediate" analyses which lie logically in between the two EXTREME analyses. This is in itself a problem for the theory since one of its basic stated goals is to seek and select a unique analysis (or solution). Once again, Chomsky and Halle's Evaluation Measure is put to task. And, as stated above, it does not provide us with an effective way of selecting the *unique solution*.

2.4. The Intermediate Analyses

The various factors can be permuted to yield intermediate analyses are listed in (26):

(26) a. limiting underlying schwas in one way or another, e.g. (i) /xðəm/ instead of /xðm/; (ii) have schwas only in grammatical morphemes; (iii) have schwas in the stem but not in grammatical morphemes, etc.

b. using versus not using boundaries of different kinds for grammatical morphemes (i.e. affixes here.).

c. permitting extrinsic rule ordering versus permitting only intrinsic rule ordering.

d. using directional rules versus non-use of such rules.

An example of an intermediate analysis (or rather strategy) is given in (27):

(27) a. underlying form of the stem: /xðəm/ 'to work'.

b. underlying form of affixes: with schwas, except /ð/, etc.

c. rules: (i) $ə \rightarrow \phi$ / ___ C V

(ii) $\phi \rightarrow ə$ / ___ C C V

d. DERIVATION OF 1ST PERSON SINGULAR:
/#xðəm+əx/ → *xðməx* → [xəðməx] (by 27i and 27ii).

Another example of an intermediate strategy is the one given in (28):[15]

---

[15]This strategy was suggested to me by Ian Maddison of U.C.L.A. I am grateful to Ian and to the participants in Prof. Fromkin's seminar for providing me with needed feedback at the initial stages of the writing of this paper.

(28) a. underlying form: /xəðəm/ 'to work'.

b. affixes with schwas, except /ð/.

c. rule: $ə \rightarrow \phi$ / ___ C V — directionality: right-to-left.

d. DERIVATION OF 1ST PERSON SINGULAR:
/#xəðəm+əx#/ → [xəðməx]

3. CONCLUSION

In conclusion, we have seen that the problem of *schwa* in Berber can be accounted for by a number of different analyses. This is not surprising and it clearly shows that merely accounting for the data, while necessary, is not a sufficient criterion for deciding between alternative solutions. Clearly one seeks some principled basis which must be determined by the theory. It should not be both a problem of accounting for *schwa* in Berber as well as "un problème de *choix*." Both the "totally abstract" and the "totally concrete" analyses were motivated by general principles. But we are still faced with the question as to which of these principles are to be accepted as theoretical constraints.

Internal formal considerations are not enough to decide. Further work in Berber as well as other languages, and further comparison of such analyses seems to be required before we can agree on the theoretical constraints. In addition to formal comparisons it appears that we must seek external verifications of the theory which will depend on such "performance" factors as perceptual strategies, storage capacity of the brain, mental generalizing abilities, etc. Until we find such evidence the linguist is left with choosing the solution which appears to be the most intuitively satisfying. I find the concrete solution more satisfactory in this case because of the ad-hoc nautre of the abstract analysis. But using this criterion is not really satisfactory. Clearly, the theory is still deficient. Hopefully, descriptive work such as is outlined here will provide some of the necessary input required for revising and further constraining phonological theory.

BIBLIOGRAPHY

Abdel Massih, Ernest T. 1968. *Tamazight Verb Structure: a generative approach.* Bloomington: Indiana University Publications.

Basset, André. 1929. *La langue berbère, morphologie, le verbe.* Paris: Leroux.

__________. 1952. *La langue berbère.* Oxford: International African Institute.

Campbell, Lyle. 1973. "Extrinsic ordering lives," (Ms.) Bloomington: Indiana University Linguistics Club.

Chomsky, N. and M. Halle. 1968. *The Sound Pattern of English.* New York: Harper and Row.

De Foucauld, (Rev.). 1920. *Notes pour servir à un essai de grammaire touarègue.* Algiers: Carbonel.

Greenberg, Joseph. 1966. *Language Universals.* The Hague: Mouton.

Hale, Kenneth. 1971. "Deep-surface canonical disparities in relation to analysis and change: an Australian example," (Ms.) To appear in *Current Trends in Linguistics*, Vol. XL, ed. by T. Sebeok et al. The Hague: Mouton.

Hooper, Joan. 1973. *Aspects of Natural Generative Phonology.* Unpublished doctoral dissertation, University of California, Los Angeles.

Howard, Irwin. 1973. *A Directional Theory of Rule Application in Phonology.* Bloomington: Indiana University Linguistics Club.

Johnson, Douglas. 1970. *Formal Aspects of Phonological Description*, in *Project on Linguistic Analysis*, No. 11. UC Berkeley: California, published again in 1972, as Monographs on Linguistic Analysis, 3. The Hague: Mouton.

Kiparsky, Paul. 1971. "Historical Linguistics" in *A Survey of Linguistic Science*, ed. by W.O. Dingwall. College Park, Md. Linguistics Program, University of Maryland.

Koutsoudas, Andreas, et alia. 1974. "The application of phonological rules," *Language* 50: 1-28.

Laoust, Emile. 1918. *Etude sur le dialècte des Ntifa*. Paris: Leroux.

Lehmann, Winfred P. 1952. *Proto-Indo-European Phonology*. Austin: The University of Texas Press, and Linguistic Society of America.

Penchoen, Thomas G. 1973. *Tamaziɣt of the Ayt Ndhir*. In Afroasiatic Dialects, Vol. 1, Berber, ed. by W. Leslau and T.G. Penchoen. Los Angeles: Undena Publications.

Prasse, Karl. 1960. "Notes sur la langue touarègue." *Acta Orientalia*. Copenhagen. Vol. XXV: 43-111.

Saib, Jilali. "The treatment of geminates: evidence from Berber," (Ms.) Paper read at the Annual Meeting of L.S.A. Dec. 1973.

Vennemann, Theo. 1972. "Rule inversion," *Lingua* 29: 209-242.

____________. 1973. "Phonological concreteness in natural generative grammar." (Ms.) U.C.L.A.

SOURCES AND MONOGRAPHS ON THE ANCIENT NEAR EAST

Editors: Giorgio Buccellati, Marilyn Kelly Buccellati, Piotr Michalowski

These two series make available original documents in English translation (*Sources*) and important studies by modern scholars (*Monographs*) as a contribution to the study of history, religion, literature, art and archaeology of the Ancient Near East. Inexpensive and flexible in format, they are meant to serve the specialist by bringing within easy reach basic publications often in updated versions, to provide imaginative educational outlets for undergraduate and graduate courses, and to reach the interested segments of the educated lay audience.

General Subscription – For a prepayment of $10 the subscriber selects random issues from within the entire system as desired, up to a total of 200 pages. The subscriber is also entitled to (1) periodical lists of abstracts from both series, and (2) reservation to given categories to be specified by the subscriber (e.g. Assyriology or Egyptology).

Library Subscription – the subscription price is $8 for Volume 1 of either the *Sources* or the *Monographs.* A volume will average 200 pages. Periodicity in the order of appearance of fascicles is not predetermined, but a volume will normally be completed within one year.

Sources from the Ancient Near East

Volume 1

- 1. *The Akkadian Namburbi Texts: an Introduction.* By R. I. Caplice. 24 pp., $1.00
- 2. *Balag-Compositions: Sumerian Lamentation Liturgies of the Second and First Millennium B.C.* By M. E. Cohen. 32 pp., $2.40

In preparation:

- ○ *The Epic of Erra.* By L. Cagni.

Monographs on the Ancient Near East

Volume 1

- 1. *The Sumerian Temple City.* By A. Falkenstein. Introduction and translation by M. Dej. Ellis. 21 pp., 95¢
- 2. *Three Essays on the Sumerians.* By B. Landsberger. Introduction and translation by M. Dej. Ellis. 18 pp., 90¢
- 3. *Structure of Society and State in Early Dynastic Sumer.* By I. B. Diakonoff. Introduction by M. Desrochers 16 pp., 65¢
- 4. *The Conceptual Autonomy of the Babylonian World.* By B. Landsberger. Translation by Th. Jacobsen, B. Foster and H. von Siebenthal. Introduction by Th. Jacobsen. 16 pp., $1.10

In preparation:

- ○ *Ebla in the Period of the Amorite Dynasty and the Dynasty of Agede: Recent Archaeological Discoveries of Tell Mardikh.* By P. Matthiae.
- ○ *Cuneiform Texts of the 3rd Millennium in Old-Canaanite from the 1974 Season at Tell Mardikh = Ebla.* By G. Pettinato.

Volume 2

- ○ *Tales of the Old Gods and Other Essays.* By T. Jacobsen.

AFROASIATIC DIALECTS

A series of grammars providing concise descriptions of individual languages within the Afroasiatic family, and directed to scholars and students in the given language areas as well as in linguistics.

Editors: Wolf Leslau and Thomas G. Penchoen

- Volume 1 (Berber). *Tamazight of the Ayt Ndhir.* By Thomas G. Penchoen. 124 pp. $8.50.
- Volume 2 (Ancient Egyptian). *Middle Egyptian.* By John B. Callender. 150 pp. $10.00.

In preparation:

- ○ Volume 3 (Semitic). *Damascus Arabic.* By Arne Ambros.

BIBLIOTHECA MESOPOTAMICA

Primary sources and interpretive analyses for the study of Mesopotamian civilization and its influences from late prehistory to the end of the cuneiform tradition.

- Volume 1. *Old Sumerian and Old Akkadian Texts in Philadelphia Chiefly from Nippur. Part 1. Literary and Lexical Texts and the Earliest Administrative Documents from Nippur.* By Aage Westenholz. xii-210 pp., 3 plates. $18.50 (hardbound), $12 (softbound).
- Volume 2. *Babylonian Planetary Omens. Part 1. The Venus Tablet of Ammiṣaduqa.* By Erica Reiner in collaboration with David Pingree. iv-60 pp. $6.75 (softbound).
- Volume 3. *Inscriptions from Al-Hiba–Lagash: The First and Second Seasons.* By Robert D. Biggs. vi-45 pp., 2 plates.

In preparation:

- ○ *The Legacy of Sumer.* Edited by D. Schmandt-Besserat.
- ○ *The Economic Role of the Crown in the Old Babylonian Period.* By Norman Yoffee.
- ○ *Seals and Sealings in Ancient Mesopotamia.* By McGuire Gibson and Robert D. Biggs.
- ○ *Old Sumerian and Old Akkadian Texts in Philadelphia.* By Aage Westenholz.
  Part 2. Late Sargonic Administrative Texts from Nippur: 'Akkadian' Texts, Legal Documents and the Onion Archive.
  Part 3. Late Sargonic Administrative Texts from Nippur: Ration Lists and Miscellaneous Accounts.
  Part 4. Presargonic and Sargonic Administrative Texts from Fara and Ur.